AF270409

WI-FI

Published in 2025 by **Cheriton Children's Books**
1 Bank Drive West, Shrewsbury, Shropshire, SY3 9DJ

First Edition

Author: Kelly Roberts
Designer: Paul Myerscough
Editor: Jennifer Sanderson
Proofreader: Amy Strauss
Consultant: David Hawksett, BSc

Picture credits: Cover: Shutterstock/Grindstone Media Group (t), Shutterstock/Asharkyu (l), Shutterstock/Suwin66 (r), Shutterstock/Makistock (b). Inside: p4: Shutterstock/Monkey Business Images, p5: Shutterstock/Vasin Lee, p6: Shutterstock/Diego Cervo, p8: Shutterstock/DimaBerlin, p9: Shutterstock/PeopleImages.com/Yuri A, p10: Shutterstock/Dean Drobot, p11: Wikimedia Commons/MGM, p12: Shutterstock/Casezy Idea, p13: Shutterstock/Diego Cervo, p14: Shutterstock/Asharkyu, p15: Shutterstock/Photoongraphy, p16: Shutterstock/Goodluz, p17: Shutterstock/Gorodenkoff, p18: Shutterstock/Lenscap Photography, p19: Shutterstock/Kaspars Grinvalds, p20: Shutterstock/Mangostar, p21: Shutterstock/Featureflash Photo Agency, p22b: Shutterstock/Oleg Elkov, p22t: Shutterstock/Ground Picture, p23: Flickr/European Patent Office, p24: Wikimedia Commons/Napoleon Sarony, p25b: Wikimedia Commons/National Portrait Gallery, p25t: Wikimedia Commons/Evert F. Baumgardner, p27: Shutterstock/New Africa, p28: Shutterstock/Aphelleon, p29: Shutterstock/John M. Chase, p30: Shutterstock/Suwin66, p31: Shutterstock/Metamorworks, p32: Shutterstock/Monkey Business Images, p33b: Shutterstock/PitukTV, p33t: Wikimedia Commons/SATorchi, p34: Shutterstock/NicoElNino, p36: Shutterstock/GaudiLab, p37: Shutterstock/Yalcin Sonat, p38: Shutterstock/Zurijeta, p39: Shutterstock/Maxshot.PL, p40: Shutterstock/Diego Thomazini, p41: Shutterstock/Anton27, p42: Shutterstock/Fizkes, p43: Wikimedia Commons/TechCrunch, p44: Shutterstock/Gorodenkoff, p45: Shutterstock/John T.

Printed in China

Please visit our website,
www.cheritonchildrensbooks.com
to see more of our high-quality books.

CONTENTS

THE WI-FI STORY

Today, we know that we can turn on our laptops, tablets, and cell phones, and within seconds we will be connected to the Internet. Much of the time, we do not need to plug in cables or wires because there is a Wi-Fi "hotspot" nearby. Wireless networks, or Wi-Fi, let us surf the web, watch videos, or listen to music without being at a fixed computer.

Our Wireless World

The technology used to develop the Wi-Fi system that we use today is an advanced version of radio technology that has existed for more than 100 years. The technology used specifically to connect to the Internet wirelessly was invented in the 1980s and 1990s. However, the term "Wi-Fi" came into use only in 1999. It was invented to try to get more people to begin using the technology. It certainly sounds a lot better than the technology's official title, which is IEEE 802.11b Direct Sequence!

Smartphones come with Wi-Fi connectivity as standard. There are Wi-Fi hotspots all around us, including in schools and colleges, so we can be online almost all the time.

A Technology That Changed the World

Wi-Fi is the process of connecting to the Internet without cables. The same data that would normally be sent to and from your computer or telephone using wires is sent through the air instead. This is done using two or more electronic devices that can send and receive data as radio waves. Radio waves are invisible waves of energy, which can carry sound, pictures, and other forms of electronic information through the air over long distances (see page 6–7). In this book we'll explore the history of Wi-Fi, how it has changed your world, and the brilliant scientists behind this incredible invention.

HOW HIGH-TECH CHANGED THE WORLD

We use Wi-Fi in our day-to-day lives. Car keys that allow drivers to lock and unlock their vehicles by pressing a button also use a technology that is very similar to Wi-Fi technology. When you use the Internet on your phone or tablet at home, you are using Wi-Fi. The technology has made it possible for us to freely communicate, entertain ourselves, and work almost anywhere. Wi-Fi has transformed our world.

Understanding Radio Waves

To understand how Wi-Fi works, you need to know a little more about radio waves and how they work. Radio waves are a form of electromagnetic energy. They are created using a simple electrical process and can be used to send information, such as sound, moving pictures, and computer data, over long distances.

Ups and Downs

We cannot see radio waves, but if we could, they would look like a continuous wavy line with several peaks (the high points of the wave) and troughs (the low points of the wave). These peaks and troughs are exactly the same amplitude, or same size. There are many different types of radio wave. For example, microwaves are used for heating and cooking food in microwave ovens and for making and receiving cell phone calls.

Watching movies or making video calls can use a lot of Wi-Fi data. Because Wi-Fi uses radio waves, its signal can easily pass through walls.

Microwaves are ultra-high-frequency radio waves (UHF). Submarines use ultra-low-frequency (ULF) radio waves for communication. The radio waves used in wireless networking and other radio uses are sine waves.

Carrying the Data

The radio sine waves from a home Internet hotspot are weak. They are strong enough to travel only up to around 330 feet (100 m). However, because Wi-Fi signals must only travel short distances, using sine waves means the waves can carry a lot of information. This is why we can "stream" high-definition movies directly to our computers, tablets, or smartphones.

Frequency of Waves

The distances between the peaks and troughs of sine waves depend on the frequency of the wave. Lower-frequency radio waves are perfect for sending information over longer distances. However, this is possible only if the equipment that creates and sends the radio waves is powerful (such as a radio transmitter), otherwise they can send data only a short distance.

HIGH-TECH HISTORY

Just outside Galesburg, North Dakota, stands the KRDK-TV mast, which broadcasts television signals across thousands of square miles (sq km) of the surrounding area. To reach homes in such a wide area, its antenna transmits at 285 kW. It is a steel tower with a lattice structure reaching 2,060 feet (628 m) in height. Since its completion in 1966 it has collapsed and been rebuilt twice! It is the tallest structure anywhere in the United States and is the seventh-tallest in the world.

Picking up Signals

For many years after the discovery of radio waves, scientists focused on broadcasting, or sending, radio signals over long distances. To do this, they invented powerful transmitters, which are types of antenna. These signals could be picked up using a receiver antenna, such as a portable radio or a television aerial.

Communicating in Two Ways

The system used to broadcast radio signals using a receiver is known as one-way communication. In this system, only one end of the link is communicating or broadcasting, while the other is simply receiving. A wireless keyboard or mouse works using one-way communication—a click or key press makes a computer respond. A system called "two-way communication" allows us to send and receive radio waves at the same time, so we can communicate in two ways.

Simple Tech

The technology behind two-way communication is simple. All it requires are devices that can send and receive radio waves. These devices can turn sound, pictures, or computer data into radio waves before sending them out into the world. They can also receive radio waves and turn them back into sound, pictures, or computer data. Wireless networking used in computer Wi-Fi connections is a great example of two-way communication. When you are connected to the Internet using Wi-Fi, your computer, tablet, or smartphone is constantly sending and receiving data in the form of radio waves.

The walkie-talkie began life as a backpack containing a two-way radio transceiver, which is any device that can be both a transmitter and a receiver. It was developed for military use during World War II (1939–1945), to help soldiers communicate while on the move. Today, walkie-talkies are handheld and can be smaller than smartphones. They are particularly useful in settings such as construction sites or visitor attractions, where one person can instantly alert and instruct a whole team using a push-to-talk button. Walkie-talkies allow for immediate communication and safety monitoring.

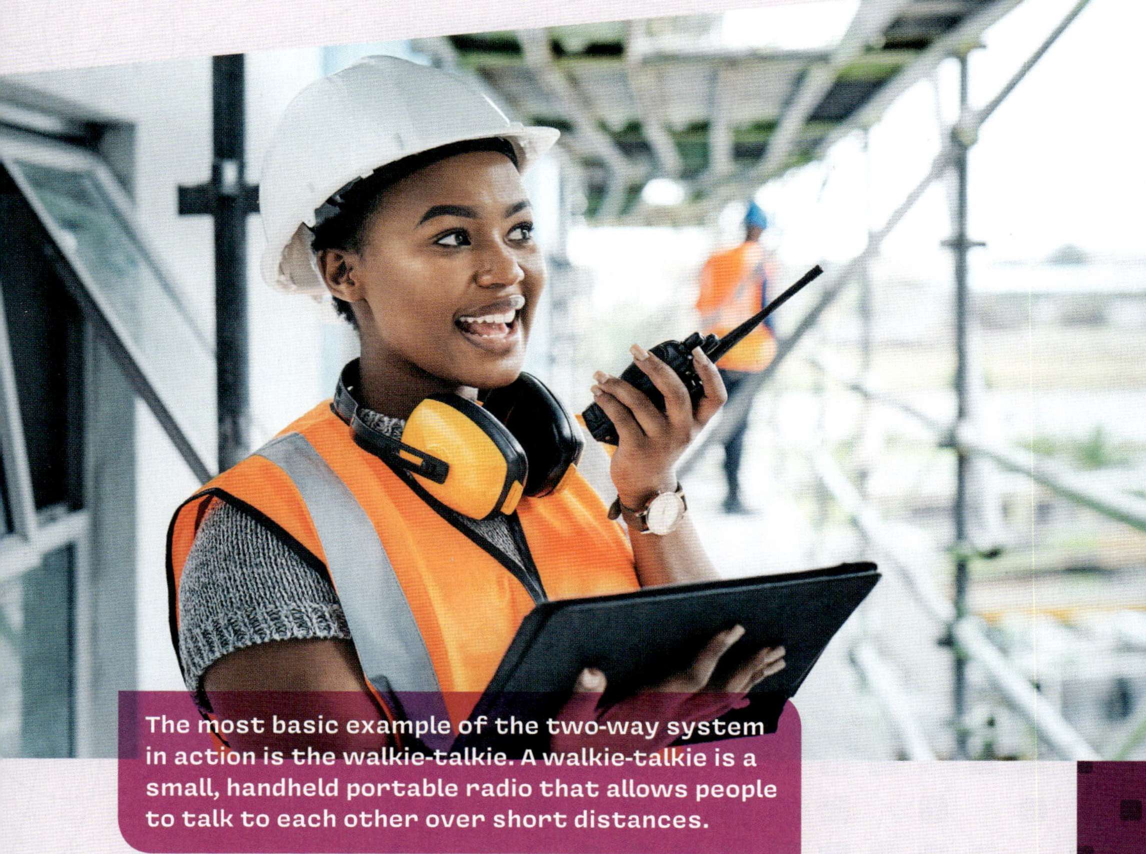

The most basic example of the two-way system in action is the walkie-talkie. A walkie-talkie is a small, handheld portable radio that allows people to talk to each other over short distances.

Understanding Frequency

From Wi-Fi computer networking to walkie-talkie radios and our smartphones, all two-way wireless devices that use radio waves send and receive information in very similar ways. But how do all these devices successfully communicate given the vast number of wireless devices in use today?

Traveling as Waves

Light and electrical signals all travel around the world and the universe as waves. Together, these forms of energy make up the electromagnetic spectrum. Light is the only part of the spectrum that we can see. The part of the spectrum that can be used by radio waves is called the radio spectrum. To ensure that all systems that use radio waves are accommodated in the radio spectrum, each is given its own narrow space, called a frequency range. By law, devices must send (and receive, if they can do so) radio waves only on their own frequency.

Sharing the Space

There is a vast number of frequencies within the radio spectrum, but it is not infinite. At some point, there will be no space left for new systems. However, to date, we have not run out of space because different forms of technology broadcast on different frequencies. For example, AM radio is broadcast from 535 kilohertz to 1,700 kilohertz (thousands of radio waves per second). FM radio stations broadcast in a range of frequencies between 88 and 108 megahertz (millions of radio waves per second). Wi-Fi devices are more effective— they communicate on frequencies between 2.4 and 5 gigahertz (billions of radio waves per second).

Hopping Around

Many modern Wi-Fi devices use a system called "frequency hopping" to guarantee the user a good signal. This means that the device can flick between different radio frequencies within their range on the spectrum to ensure that the connection remains stable.

HIGH-TECH STARS WHO CHANGED THE WORLD

HEDY LAMARR

The actress Hedy Lamarr (1914–2000) was born in Vienna, then part of Austria-Hungary, before moving to the United States and becoming a Hollywood movie star. Lamarr was also an accomplished inventor and worked on her ideas even while filming movies. She had previously been married to a weapons dealer, and was aware that navies were considering radio control to guide torpedoes. Lamarr developed an idea that would use changing the remote-control frequency, or "frequency hopping," to prevent an enemy jamming the signal. Lamarr and co-inventor George Antheil were awarded a patent for their invention, which they gave to the US navy for free.

Turning Data into Waves

The process used by Wi-Fi devices to connect to the Internet is like that used by two-way radios. However, instead of sound being turned into radio waves and back again, it is computer data. To create a connection to the Internet, your Wi-Fi-enabled device, for example, a laptop, tablet computer, or smartphone, needs to communicate with another device, called a wireless router. The wireless router is connected to the Internet using a special kind of wire called an Ethernet cable.

Adaptors at Work

When you switch on your laptop, tablet, or smartphone, it attempts to connect to the Internet through the router. It does this using a device called a wireless adapter. This is a tiny antenna capable of turning instructions in the form of computer data (for example, a request to send an email) into a radio signal. The router receives this signal, turns it back into computer data, and acts on the instructions. Once it has done this, it then turns the computer data back into radio waves, which it sends to your Wi-Fi device. The device's wireless adapter then receives the signal and turns it back into computer data. This entire process takes only a fraction of a second.

Listening to Music

When you are listening to music over the Internet using Wi-Fi, your computer is constantly communicating with the wireless router. Both devices can send and receive huge amounts of data very quickly, more than enough to download a 4-minute MP3 in just a few seconds.

HOW HIGH-TECH CHANGED THE WORLD

MP3 is the popular format for digital music files. It was developed in the late 1980s and was standardized in 1991. The first software that could play MP3s on computers, WinPlay3, was launched in 1995. MP3s compress, or reduce in size, sound files by removing any frequencies that are not audible, or cannot be heard. They led to a revolution in personal music players, which previously needed to be physically loaded with a single album on a cassette tape or compact disc.

MP3 has made it possible to listen to music wherever you are, either at home, traveling, or even while exercising outdoors.

CHAPTER 2

HOW WIRELESS NETWORKS WORK

Connecting to the Internet using Wi-Fi is made possible not just by radio waves and wireless adapters, but also by a vast global network of underground and submarine, or below-water, cables. Without these cables, we would not be able to connect to the Internet on the move.

A Gateway to the World

If you look at the back of a wireless router, you will notice a thick, rubber-coated cable plugged in to it. This is an Ethernet cable. This cable is the wireless router's gateway to the vast network of communications cables that carry computer data around the world. Underground and submarine communications cables crisscross neighborhoods, towns, cities, states, countries, and even oceans. Together, they form the wide area network (WAN). Without the WAN, the Internet would not work.

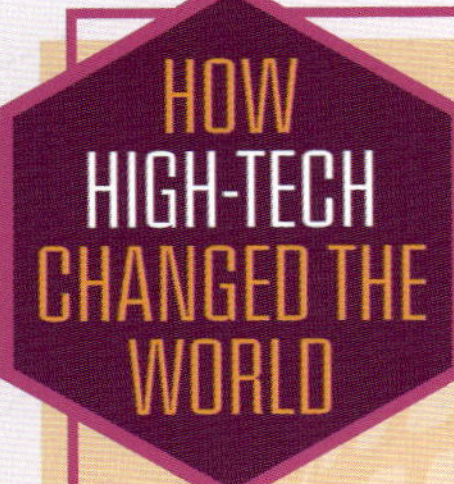

Today's underground cables use a system called fiber optics. In this system, data is turned into pulses of light, which can be beamed through the cables at superfast speeds. It can take just a few hundredths of a second for a fiber-optic signal to travel from one side of the world to the other. Many fiber-optic cables have also been laid on the seafloor. The first section was completed in 1996, which crossed the Pacific Ocean. Today, there are more than 400 submarine fiber-optic cables, with a combined length of around 800,000 miles (1.3 million km). They too allow data to be sent around the world at incredible speeds.

Billions of Computers

The WAN joins together billions of computers around the world. Every website is "hosted" on a computer somewhere in the world, usually a large storage computer called a server. When you type in a website address and press the return key, your computer, tablet, or smartphone sends a request for access to the host computer. Even when you connect wirelessly using a router, this request is sent down cables across the WAN, until it reaches its destination. The response to your request will come back down the same cables, be turned into radio waves by your wireless router, and is then beamed through the air to your device.

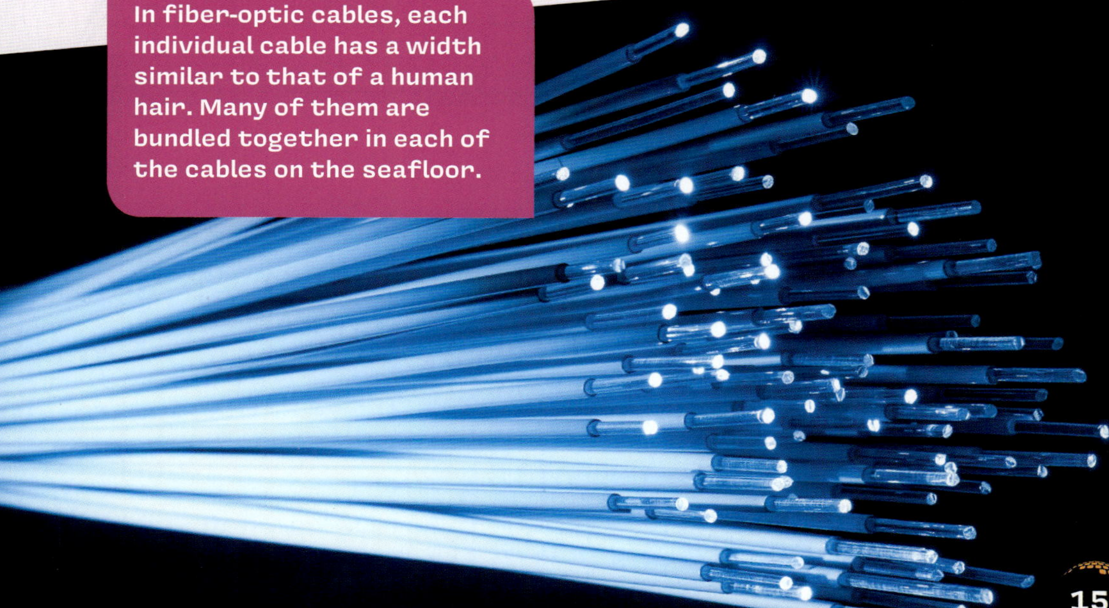

When you log-in to a WLAN your device remembers the details including the network password. This means you will automatically connect to the WLAN at a friend's house if your device has been previously connected.

Connecting Local Areas

The WAN that carries computer data around the world is a collection of a lot of smaller networks. The smallest of these are called local area networks (LANs). These are the networks used in homes, schools, colleges, and offices.

Sharing One Connection

A LAN allows many computers, and other electronic devices, to share a single connection to the Internet. Before wireless technology, the computers in a LAN were connected to a single Internet router using Ethernet cables. Today, most LANs operate using wireless technology.

Using a wireless router, the devices can share the same Internet connection without plugging in cables. This is known as a wireless local area network, or WLAN.

Internet Annoyance

Using a WLAN, it is possible for several different wireless devices to connect to the Internet at the same time. This is because the wireless router can communicate with many different devices at the same time. However, the router can send and receive only a certain amount of data at any given time. This is why the Internet can sometimes seem slow when a lot of people are connected to the same WLAN. Check when the busy times are where you live—is there a pattern to them?

Wireless Wonder

In addition to connecting to the Internet, WLANs have other uses. Once you have set up a WLAN in your home, you can use it to transfer documents and files between different computers in the same WLAN, or access a shared music collection stored on a shared computer.

HOW HIGH-TECH CHANGED THE WORLD

In the late 1990s, a new type of event gained popularity: the LAN party. The parties began when a small group of friends brought their computers and gathered at one person's home, usually for a night or a weekend. With all machines connected to that home's LAN, every party member could play games against each other. Today, LAN parties also exist as massive, organized events in which thousands of gamers gather and connect their computers over a LAN.

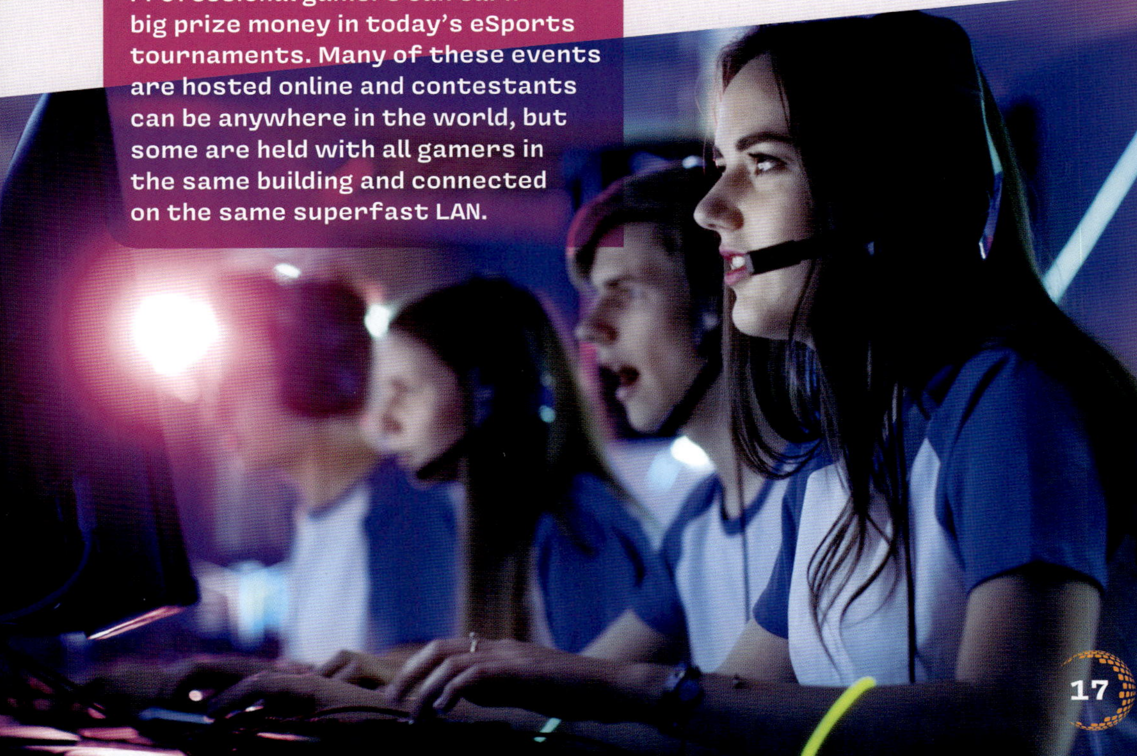

Professional gamers can earn big prize money in today's eSports tournaments. Many of these events are hosted online and contestants can be anywhere in the world, but some are held with all gamers in the same building and connected on the same superfast LAN.

Before the smartphone revolution, people used their cell phones mostly for voice calls and texting.

What Are Hotspots?

If you could connect only to your own WLAN, wireless technology would be of limited use. However, there are now Wi-Fi "hotspots" all over towns and cities, from libraries and restaurants to airports and railroad stations, making it possible to connect to the Internet using WLAN almost anywhere you go.

Hitting the Hotspot

Wi-Fi hotspots exist when the owners of a business or building offer access to their wireless router, often free of charge. Computer, tablet, and smartphone users can then connect to the Internet during their time in that building or public space. Usually, buildings or businesses that offer a Wi-Fi hotspot service advertise the fact. Often, you will need to enter a password to gain access to the network, but this is also usually advertised by providers.

Happy to Share

Each Wi-Fi hotspot is, in fact, a WLAN, just like the one you may have at home or school. However, the difference is that the people who own the network are happy for many different people to use it. They pay the cost of the Internet connection so users do not have to. You would not be quite so pleased if people used your home WLAN for free, rather than paying for their own!

Your Own Hotspot

If you or someone you know has an iPhone or Android phone, you can create your own hotspot. To do this, you need to turn on the "personal hotspot" option in the "preferences" section. When this is turned on, the iPhone will become a wireless router. You can then share your iPhone's wireless connection with other devices, such as a laptop or iPad. This is especially convenient if you are out and need the Internet.

Smartphones need to be large enough for easy use and to house the big battery that takes up much of their internal space.

HOW HIGH-TECH CHANGED THE WORLD

The first iPhone, introduced by Apple in 2007, marked a major milestone in cell phone technology. Its powerful processor, high-resolution and color touch screen, and a wide variety of smart applications, or apps, made the phone far more like a pocket computer than any previous phone. Later models, including phones running the rival operating system Android, incorporated more powerful cameras, along with wireless charging, fingerprint login, and other security features. Before the iPhone, cell phones were becoming smaller, but the smartphone revolution has led to demand for larger screens and more functions.

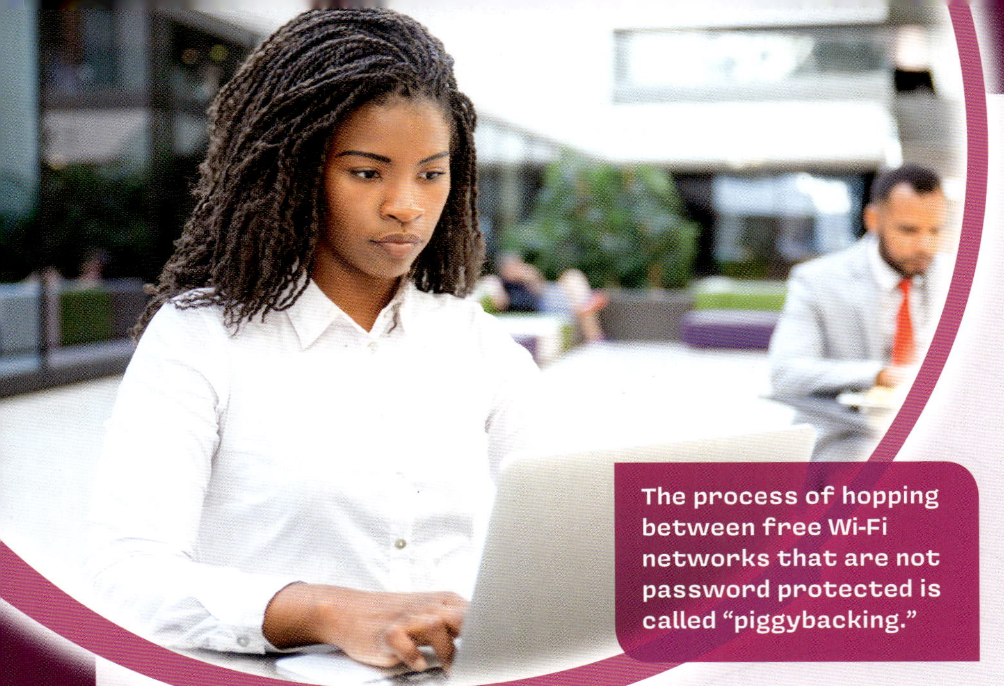

Security Matters

If you are using a wireless network, it is very important that you protect yourself when working online. This means taking security measures to make sure that criminals cannot get hold of your personal information. By adding password protection to your WLAN, people will need to correctly enter a password before they can connect to your home WLAN.

Safe and Secure

Early wireless routers were not very secure, and users complained to the manufacturers that their inbuilt security systems were not good enough. Thanks to years of development, wireless routers are now very secure. They use several systems to protect their connections from being hijacked by criminals.

Password Protected

The most widely used system to protect WLANs is called Wi-Fi Protected Access 2, or WPA2. To connect to a WLAN that is protected by WPA2, you need to enter a password. Once you do this, you will be granted access. Because there is a huge number of possible passwords, this makes it a lot more difficult for criminals to "hack" into your Wi-Fi network.

Access Control

Another popular Wi-Fi security system is Media Access Control (MAC). Every computer in the world has a unique MAC address. If you know the address of your computer, and other users of your WLAN, you can make your router grant access only to these computers.

HIGH-TECH HISTORY

In 1999, Apple's boss Steve Jobs (1955–2011) demonstrated on stage that his laptop was wirelessly connected to the Internet by holding it up and passing a hula-hoop over it. In 2003, the technology company Intel launched its Centrino chips for laptops, which have inbuilt Wi-Fi as standard. On stage at its launch, Intel's vice president Pat Gelsinger presented a Centrino laptop, which was connected to the Internet via an Ethernet cable, and was streaming online video. Gelsinger took out a kitchen meat cleaver and severed the cable! The audience could see the video continue uninterrupted, even with no connecting wires and no external wireless adapter or dongle. Both events were huge moments in Internet connection technology.

Steve Jobs was a tech pioneer who used the capabilities of Wi-Fi to expand Apple and its technology.

Devices That Talk to Each Other

The technology that allows electronic devices to send and receive data as radio waves has more uses than simply connecting to the Internet. It is now possible for some electronic devices to communicate with each other, without setting up a WLAN.

Gaming Networks

Ad hoc Wi-Fi transmission is a system in which two electronic devices communicate directly using wireless technology. One of the most popular uses of this is in the "wireless ad hoc network" mode offered by handheld game consoles such as the Nintendo DS and PlayStation Portable (PSP). This mode allows gamers in the same room to play networked games against each other. For ad hoc wireless transmission to work, each handheld console must wirelessly connect to the others using its inbuilt wireless adapter.

Connecting with Bluetooth

Another form of direct wireless networking is a system called Bluetooth. Bluetooth was invented in the 1990s, to allow electronic devices such as cell phones, laptops, and digital cameras to communicate with each other. Just like Wi-Fi, Bluetooth uses radio waves to send and receive data. However, the radio waves it uses are much shorter than those used in Wi-Fi, so connections can only take place between devices that are at most just a few tens of feet apart.

The Nintendo Switch was launched in 2017. It has both Bluetooth and Wi-Fi connectivity.

One of the most popular uses of Bluetooth technology is the hands-free headset worn by drivers. When a driver's cell phone rings, they press a button on the headset to answer the phone. Using radio waves, the phone then transfers the call to and from the headset via Bluetooth.

HIGH-TECH STARS WHO CHANGED THE WORLD

JAAP HAARTSEN

Dutch electrical engineer and inventor Jaap Haartsen was inducted in the National Inventors Hall of Fame in 2015 for his work on the creation of Bluetooth. Haartsen's endeavors created a standard for the way devices connect over a personal area network (PAN). Before 2015, wireless keyboards, mice, headsets, and other devices were already available, but used their own frequencies and risked losing connection due to interference. Devices for personal computers were becoming more diverse, so Bluetooth was designed to reduce the clutter of cables around a workstation. Bluetooth radio has a short range of up to around 33 feet (10 m).

CHAPTER 3

BIG CHANGES WITH WI-FI

The wireless technology that makes so much difference to our lives today is the result of more than 100 years of research and development. Without certain key discoveries, today's superfast Wi-Fi connections would not be possible.

No Practical Application!

The development of wireless technology began in 1876, when a German scientist named Heinrich Rudolf Hertz (1857–1894) proved the existence of radio waves. However, Hertz thought his discovery had little merit and no practical application. Hertz could not have been more wrong! By 1892, a Croatian scientist named Nikola Tesla (1856–1943) had demonstrated that radio waves could be transmitted. Tesla had figured out that it was possible to artificially create and send radio waves out into the world.

HIGH-TECH STARS WHO CHANGED THE WORLD

NIKOLA TESLA

Nikola Tesla is the father of wireless technology. His wireless telegraphy system later became the basis of radio broadcasting. In 1898, Tesla wowed crowds in Madison Square Garden, New York City, by demonstrating the world's first radio-controlled boat. Remote-controlled toy cars, boats, and airplanes used today are based on the system Tesla invented.

By 1934, 60 percent of homes in the United States had a radio receiver. Radio stations, which broadcast music, talk, and drama, began appearing all over the world to entertain listeners.

Crossing the Atlantic

In 1901, the world changed when long-range radio broadcasting arrived. With money from investors, including inventor Thomas Edison (1847–1931), Italian scientist Guglielmo Marconi (1874–1937) sent the first radio transmission across the Atlantic Ocean. Using powerful radio transmitters in Newfoundland and Ireland, he proved that radio waves could send sound over thousands of miles.

Messages to Ships

In the very early days of radio broadcasting, few scientists believed radio signals would be used for entertainment. The first radio systems were used to send signals to ships out in the oceans. Messages were not spoken, as we would expect today, but sent as Morse code. Morse code, named for inventor Samuel Morse (1791–1872), is a series of simple electronic noises, or dots and dashes, that can be used to create words.

In 1832, while returning from Europe to the United States by ship, Samuel Morse came up with the idea of an electric telegraph upon hearing a conversation about the newly discovered electromagnet. By 1835, Morse had made his first working model of an electric telegraph.

What Is Radar?

Heinrich Rudolph Hertz did not only discover that radio waves could be transmitted, but he also discovered that they can be reflected when they hit solid objects in their path. During the 1930s and early 1940s, governments around the world conducted secret experiments to see if Hertz's discovery, made some 50 years earlier, could be used to warn of attacks from the air. The system they developed became known as radar, which is short for Radio Detection And Ranging.

Reflecting Radio Waves

The principles behind radar are simple. A powerful transmitter pointed toward the sky sends out a continuous stream of radio waves. When the radio waves hit a solid object, they are reflected, or scattered, in many directions. Some bounce back toward the transmitter. By placing a receiver device close to the transmitter, it is possible to figure out the exact position in the sky of the object that was hit.

A Military Secret

Radar systems were first put into use in World War II, when they helped the British and US forces defeat the Germans. By detecting overhead planes, the two countries' air forces could send up their own planes to shoot down the German counterparts. Since then, the use of radar has become widespread and the system is no longer a tool for just the military.

Using Radar

Today, air traffic controllers use radar to track the position of planes in the sky as they crisscross the world. Radar is also used to keep track of the world's weather systems. The United States boasts a vast network of radar stations, which are used to predict the movements of dangerous storms. This means people can be warned of an approaching storm and the necessary precautions can be taken.

Radar operators during World War II noticed their radar signals were bouncing off clouds, potentially hindering their chances of spotting enemy aircraft. Scientists soon began studying these echoes, and began to use them to study weather. Today, weather radar is highly advanced and people working in radar ground stations use the technology to tell the difference between rain, snow, and hail. They can also determine the exact location, movement direction, and intensity of any precipitation.

We all now have access to weather radar data because live, historic, and forecasted weather can be found using a computer or smartphones with apps such as Ventusky.

In Space

The discovery that radio waves could travel long distances and be reflected toward the point of their origin, has led to the development of even more cutting-edge technology in the last 50 years. One of the most significant inventions is radio astronomy. Radio astronomy is based on the principle that all objects transmit energy in the form of radio waves. There are countless objects in space. These include planets, galaxies, and stars. Many of these objects, even those that are millions of light years away, send out natural radio waves just as they emit visible light. Astronomers use large radio antennas that are powerful enough to receive their signals to help them study these objects.

Satellites in Space

Another use of radio waves developed in the last 70 years is satellite technology. Scientists realized that by placing reflective objects, known as satellites, in set points above Earth, they could bounce radio waves off them and back toward our planet. This technology has several useful applications, including satellite television.

Satellites for Television

In order for satellite television to work, pictures are turned into radio waves, and beamed to a satellite in space. The satellite then sends the radio waves back toward Earth, where they are picked up by receivers (satellite dishes) and turned back into television pictures.

Light-Years Away

In 2012, scientists used radio astronomy to discover one of the most distant objects in the universe that has been detected so far. The distant galaxy is some 13.3 billion light-years away from our planet. Each wave of light travels at a speed of 186,000 miles per second (300,000 kps), so you can only imagine how far away the most distant galaxy is!

HOW HIGH-TECH CHANGED THE WORLD

The Robert C. Byrd Green Bank Telescope (GBT) in West Virginia uses a huge radio dish that measures 328 feet (100 m) across to detect the faint natural radio waves emitted by objects in the universe. The dish is incredibly smooth—in fact, it has no blemishes or bumps taller than the thickness of five human hairs! This makes the GBT extremely sensitive, and astronomers have used it to discover amazing space objects such as pulsars, neutron stars, and a huge hydrogen gas bubble in our own galaxy.

The GBT is the largest fully-steerable radio telescope in the world.

Cell Phones Take Over

Although satellite technology has improved our lives and radio astronomy has increased our understanding of the universe, neither technology has affected our lives quite as much as cell phone technology, which allows us to communicate wherever we are in the world. Today, it is thought that there are 8 billion connected cell phones.

Using Wave Power

Cell phones use radio waves to send and receive data. Each time you make or receive a call on a cell phone or a smartphone, the data is routed around the world using a network of masts—which can send and receive radio waves—and satellites positioned above Earth.

Grids That Are Connected

The global cell phone, or cellular, network is divided into a series of small grids, or cells. Each cell has its own mast, and each mast is given its own unique radio frequency to send and receive calls. As users pass from one cell to the next, their phone automatically detects the change and tunes in to the new frequency.

Next Generation

The third-generation (3G), fourth-generation (4G), and fifth-generation (5G) cell phone networks we use today can send and receive huge amounts of computer data very quickly. The 4G network connection is 30 times faster than 3G—In fact, 4G connection is as fast as Wi-Fi.

Since 2019, 5G for cell phone networks and devices has been in use. It allows for many more devices to connect to the cell phone network, and has download speeds that are up to 100 times faster than 4G. The faster data rate is vital for emerging technologies such as self-driving automobiles. It will also be critical for surgery performed by a robot controlled remotely by a surgeon in another location. The older 3G and 2G networks are gradually being turned off as 5G coverage increases.

Eventually all cars will be self-driving. We already use the Global Positioning System (GPS) in our vehicles for navigation but Wi-Fi is also critical as it helps cars detect each other on the highway.

Creating a Wireless Connection

When computer networking became popular in the late 1980s, scientists began developing wireless connections using radio waves. Yet, however hard they tried, they could not create a clear signal and a strong connection. To make wireless networking possible, scientists would have to create a system in which a good proportion of radio waves reached their intended destination.

Any modern city is filled with radio waves, from short-range devices such as car keys, to traditional radio sets that pick up radio broadcasts. Wi-Fi hotspots are now a major part of our cities, and in use everywhere, from public places to busy offices.

Making a Breakthrough

In 1992, Australian radio astronomer John O'Sullivan made a significant breakthrough. He discovered that if you split the radio signal into a vast number of radio waves, enough waves would get through to ensure a clear signal and a good connection. O'Sullivan and his research team created a wireless adapter that could be included in laptops and wireless routers. It went on sale to computer manufacturers in 2000, and within six years more than 100 million people were regularly using Wi-Fi. Today, wireless adapters come as standard in almost all computers, smartphones, and tablets, as well as other devices such as game consoles. In little over 20 years, Wi-Fi has become the standard way to connect to the Internet.

HIGH-TECH STARS WHO CHANGED THE WORLD

JOHN O'SULLIVAN

John O'Sullivan, whose work in astronomy led to the creation of Wi-Fi, demonstrated how science and invention can be unpredictable. Discoveries that were not expected can lead to great advances in a completely different area of science and technology. O'Sullivan is currently working on technology to create Wi-Fi networks with greater ranges, lower-power use, and the ability to share connections among many connected devices. This will help future technology, in which many more devices, such as home security systems, need Internet connection to support all their features.

Despite O'Sullivan's discovery, Wi-Fi is still not quite perfect. Wireless routers have a range of up to about 330 feet (100 m) outdoors, but users will usually receive a strong signal only if they are within 165 feet (50 m) of the router. The signal will also be weaker if objects are in the way.

CHAPTER 4

USING WI-FI

The boom in wireless technology in the last few years, and in particular Wi-Fi Internet, has changed the way we live our lives. Whether we are at home, out and about, or even on vacation, Wi-Fi has made a dramatic difference to our daily lives.

Wi-Fi Rules the World!

If you think about some of the ways that people use a computer or laptop, tablet, or smartphone, and where they use these devices, you will quickly realize just how much people rely on wireless Internet connections. In an average day, people may update their status at any time of day on social networking sites such as Instagram, post something, upload pictures of themselves and friends, or watch videos on YouTube or TikTok. Whichever device people use, and wherever they do this, all these activities are only possible thanks to Wi-Fi.

As long as three or more GPS satellites are above your horizon in the sky, then your position on Earth can be calculated.

Keeping Connected

As a result of the wireless network, people are almost always connected. Smartphones will automatically connect to any Wi-Fi network that the phone recognizes. This is usually one that is free, or one that people have previously connected to by entering a password. If there is no Wi-Fi network available, people can connect to the Internet over the cellular cell phone network instead. Almost anywhere in the country, people can connect to the Internet.

Where Are You?

Have you ever wondered how your smartphone knows where you are in the world, and how people can add their location to social media posts? A smartphone does this by accessing the GPS. The GPS is a network of satellites high above Earth that can accurately locate the position of any GPS-enabled device.

HOW HIGH-TECH CHANGED THE WORLD

The GPS network has 31 operating satellites orbiting Earth 16,500 miles (26,600 km) above the planet's surface. GPS was originally restricted for use only by the US military, but was approved for civilian, or nonmilitary, use in the 1980s. Even then, its accuracy was deliberately degraded for anyone other than US forces. This rule was abandoned in 2000, and now all GPS devices have access to the same positioning accuracy as the military. That means that modern smartphones can now determine their position to within 16 feet (4.9 m).

Wi-Fi at Work

Wi-Fi has changed the way people work. Businesspeople no longer need to be based in an office building with wired access to the Internet. Today, people can do business on the move, using their laptops, tablet computers, and smartphones.

On the Move

Businesspeople who must travel a lot are served well by the wireless world. Today, most major railroad stations and airports offer free Wi-Fi access. Wi-Fi also comes as standard at many hotels and an increasing number of coffee shops, restaurants, and bars offer free Wi-Fi to their customers. If people have a laptop or a smartphone, they can work almost anywhere in the world.

Apps Are the Answer

Many apps have been developed to make doing business easier. For example, many banks now offer their customers apps that allow them to manage their money on their phones, wherever they are in the world. Many stores can also now take credit card payments using wireless card readers. These handheld devices communicate with the store's router using a secure Wi-Fi connection, which then allows communication with the customer's bank.

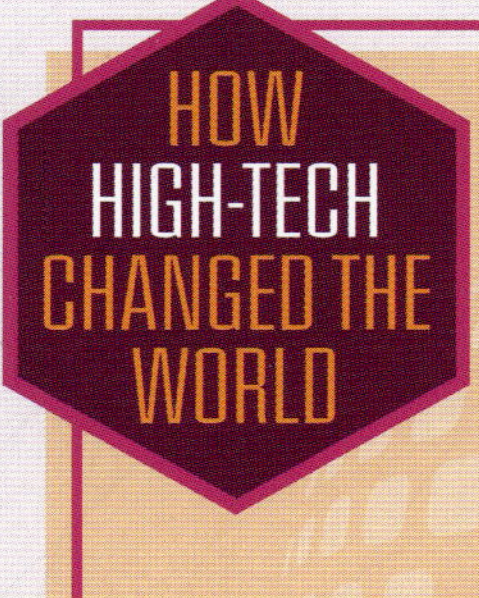

Just as Wi-Fi and Bluetooth are standards for wireless communication, Universal Serial Bus (USB) is the global standard for physical or wired connections. Before USB, a home computer needed multiple types of ports to connect keyboards, mice, printers, and audio devices. USB was first introduced in 1998, and allows both data and power to be sent to a device connected to a rectangular USB port. USB allows "plug and play," a system in which connected devices can recognize each other without needing the installation of specific software. A USB port also allows for an adapter or hub to be plugged in, allowing several devices to share one connection.

Using Dongles

Many cell phone providers also sell a device called a dongle. A dongle allows laptop users to connect to the Internet using the cellular network. Using them is very simple. All that is required is to plug the dongle into the USB port of a laptop, wait until the software loads, and click on "connect." If the user can get cell phone reception, they will be able to connect to the Internet.

USB connections come in different shapes and sizes and include Mini-USB and Micro-USB. Until now Apple iPhones have used their own connector but future models will use USB-C, the same as Android phones.

Wi-Fi and Television

Wireless technology is also changing the world of television, and specifically how we watch it. Families once gathered to watch one television in one room. Today, each family member can watch what they want, when they want, and where they want on multiple devices.

Television—24/7

Thanks to the invention of personal television recorder boxes such as TiVo, people can now watch their favorite programs at a time that suits them. This technology may seem modern, but today even greater cutting-edge television technologies are available—smartphone apps. These allow users to tell their set-top box to record a program, even if they are thousands of miles away from home. There are also apps that allow you to turn your smartphone into a remote control to change channels and other settings using your WLAN.

YouTube has opened up the world of content sharing, allowing anyone to create their own videos and then post them online.

NETFLIX

Netflix, Disney+, and other streaming services have changed how we watch television. Shows can be viewed on any device that has Wi-Fi and is within the signal bubble of a Wi-Fi router.

HIGH-TECH HISTORY

Netflix is one of the online-video-streaming services that has changed the television industry. It began in 1997, as a movie-rental service through which movies arrived as DVDs in the mail. The service then began streaming movies and television shows in 2007 and, in 2013, started to make its own content too. It now has more than 260 million subscribers across more than 190 countries worldwide, and is the favorite streaming service of almost 50 percent of Americans.

The Power of Streaming

It is now possible to create your own mini "home television network" using your computer and WLAN. Services such as iTunes and Apple television allow users to store movies and television episodes on one computer, and then transmit, or stream, the pictures to other computers, tablets, and smartphones that are connected to the WLAN.

Television on Demand

The incredibly fast speed of Wi-Fi Internet connections has also led to a rise in the popularity of television-on-demand services. These are either apps or websites, such as YouTube and Disney+, which allow you to watch programs on your laptop, smartphone, game console, or tablet. You can use these services anywhere where they are available —all you need is a suitable device and a good Wi-Fi connection.

The EA Sports soccer game FC 24 is one of the most popular games played on Xbox.

Changing the World of Gaming

It is not only the invention of online gaming that has changed the way people play games, but wireless technology has also made playing computer games a much more energetic and athletic activity. Two of the most popular game consoles of recent years, the PlayStation 5 and the Xbox Series X, owe much of their popularity to the wireless technology in each machine.

Both consoles contain wireless adapters to connect to the Internet. Both offer players the chance to play networked games against opponents from all over the world, using the Internet. Some consoles use wireless controllers that feature motion sensors. Motion sensors pick up on a player's movement and react accordingly.

Motion Sensors at Work

Motion sensors work by sending and receiving waves of invisible light, known as infrared light. In the case of game consoles, the base unit transmits waves of light, while the remote control receives them. Every time the remote detects a wave of light, it sends back the information to the base unit, using radio waves. It then updates the on-screen game.

Multiplayer Games

It is not just game consoles that have embraced the world of Wi-Fi gaming. Many games designed for smartphones and tablet computers feature wireless game modes. These allow two or more users to play multiplayer games over their home WLAN. Users do not need to connect to the Internet to play, because the wireless router acts as a bridge between two phones, laptops, or tablet computers.

HOW HIGH-TECH CHANGED THE WORLD

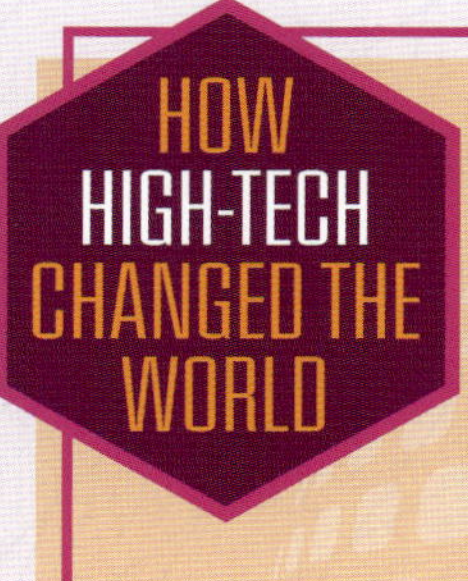

A drone is an uncrewed aerial vehicle controlled remotely by a human. The popularity of drones has increased as batteries have become lighter and longer-lasting. They are used for everything from military operations to moviemaking, and some are even classed as toys. Many drones have Wi-Fi, allowing control from a phone and live streaming from the drone's camera to the phone's screen. Racing drones are often connected by Wi-Fi to a virtual-reality (VR) headset, giving the operator the feeling of actually flying!

Because a drone uses Wi-Fi, it is necessary to keep the craft within range of the operator. Many drones also have inbuilt GPS so, if they lose Wi-Fi connection with their user, they can automatically fly back to the location they were launched from.

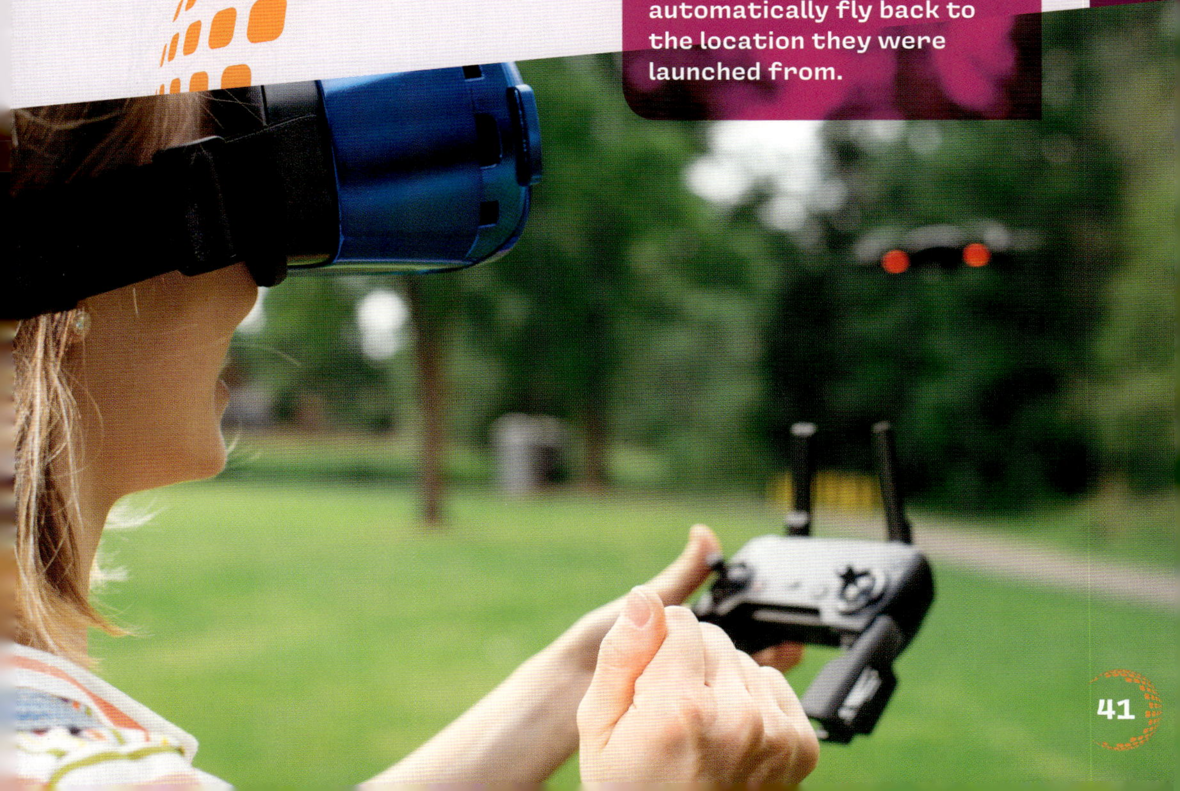

Today, a Wi-Fi connection to the Internet can handle video calls with many people at once. Video-conferencing calls have changed how people in organizations have meetings.

The Wireless Way

The advances in wireless technology in recent years have made amazing innovations possible, several that some people thought would never be possible. One of the biggest advances is video calling, which has been made popular by software applications such as Skype, Zoom, TEAMs, and Facetime. These applications allow you to make live video calls to people, or leave video messages, either over a Wi-Fi Internet connection or the cell phone network. To use these applications, all you need is a smartphone, a tablet computer, or a laptop with an inbuilt webcam.

How Video Calls Work

Video calls work because the sound from the phone's microphone and the moving pictures from its camera are turned into computer data. This data is then turned into radio waves that are sent to the Wi-Fi router or cell phone network. The process also works in reverse, so you can watch and hear others as you talk.

Music on the Move

The development of superfast wireless connections has also made listening to music on the move much easier. Now, you can stream live radio or DJ mixes on your smartphone or tablet computer, download new albums in a matter of seconds, and even broadcast your own live streams from anywhere with a Wi-Fi or cell-phone connection.

On the Go

With a Wi-Fi connection, you can also watch live television, including sports events, wherever you are. Many sports channels, such as Fox Sports and ESPN, offer special Internet subscriptions. These allow you to pay to watch the channel on your laptop, desktop computer, or tablet. Some channels even allow you to choose which sports event you watch when several events start at the same time.

HIGH-TECH STARS WHO CHANGED THE WORLD

JUSTIN KAN

Justin Kan is an Internet pioneer. In 2007, Kan and his friends launched a website named Justin.tv, in which he live-streamed his daily life. The site allowed others to create their own channels and broadcast their own live streams too. Public Wi-Fi meant people could broadcast from anywhere with a connection, not just their own home and WLAN. Justin.tv had a section devoted to gaming, which later became the popular live-streaming site Twitch.

A HIGH-TECH FUTURE

Wi-Fi as we know it today did not exist 30 years ago. Today, it enhances our lives by keeping us connected to the world through the Internet 24 hours a day. Whether we want to play games, chat with friends, share photos, manage our money, or choose what television programs or movies to watch, Wi-Fi allows us to do it without the need to plug in a device.

Speed Is the Key

The pace of this change has almost been as fast as the fiber-optic cables that carry computer data around the world at the speed of light. It is the speed of the connection more than the invention of Wi-Fi technology that has enabled our wireless world. The speed of the connection between your computer and wireless router is important, but without a quick Internet connection, it would be irrelevant. Fast Internet means fast Wi-Fi, and ultimately this enables all the activities we have come to expect, such as quickly uploading pictures and movies and watching videos online.

Thanks to Wi-Fi, future smart cities will feature cars with inbuilt traffic-monitoring technology (see opposite).

Internet over Wi-Fi is transforming our cities for the better. In the future this continuous connectivity will spread to include rural areas, thanks to Internet via satellites. Eventually, all devices might get their connection directly from satellites orbiting Earth, and we may even no longer need Wi-Fi!

The Best Is Yet to Come

Wi-Fi is still a new technology. While the power of radio waves has been used for more than 100 years, it is only since 2000 that we have enjoyed wireless Internet connections. Like any new technology, Wi-Fi is always developing. In years to come, we will be able to send more computer data at a far quicker pace than we do today. That means even better-quality videos and music that will stream even faster. Better, faster connections will also mean smartphone apps that push the technology to its very limits.

HOW HIGH-TECH CHANGED THE WORLD

By 2050, two-thirds of all people will live in cities. To deal with this growth, cities will need to become smarter. Smart-city projects have already been completed in cities including Seoul, South Korea, and Singapore, and Wi-Fi is often central to them. Traffic congestion will be monitored in much more detail when all cars have Wi-Fi and are communicating with a city-wide network. A dashboard camera could alert first responders instantly if it is on the network and witnessed a crash. More efficient electricity use, cleaner air, and happier citizens are some of the main aims of smart cities. None of this would be possible without the invention of Wi-Fi.

GLOSSARY

aerial a piece of electronic equipment capable of receiving and transmitting radio waves

antennas pieces of electronic equipment capable of receiving and transmitting radio waves

apps short for application software —these programs tell a computer or other device to do something

Bluetooth a system created to allow cell phones, and other devices, to communicate with each other without the need for cables

computer data information sent and received by computers or similar electronic devices

dongle a device that connects users to the Internet over the cell phone network rather than a Wi-Fi network

download the process of transferring something from the Internet onto your personal computer or smartphone

Ethernet cable a type of cable used for connecting or networking computers

fiber-optic cables cables made up of many long, thin strands of plastic or glass that turn information into pulses of light, rather than electrical signals

Internet the network of smaller computer networks that join to form one single global network

radio astronomy searching the universe using radio waves

radio waves invisible waves of energy that can pass through the air. Radio waves are used to transmit computer data, sound, and pictures

smartphones cell phones with additional computing power

software a computer application or program designed to do a specific task, for example, send email, edit photos, or record music

tablets touchscreen computers, such as iPads

transmit to send information

transmitter something that transmits information, often in the form of radio waves or electrical signals

Universal Serial Bus (USB) a type of wired connection between devices to transmit data and power

upload the process of transferring something from your computer, smartphone, or tablet to a website or Internet server

webcam a small video camera that connects to your computer and allows you to send and receive video messages or live-stream from your computer

wireless technology that allows the exchange of information, or communication between people, but does not require traditional cables or wires

wireless local area network (WLAN) the combination of a wireless router and Wi-Fi-enabled devices that allows you to connect to the Internet wirelessly

wireless router a device that acts as a gateway between Wi-Fi devices and the Internet

Books

Mabry Gordon, Sherri. *Internet Security and You* (The Promise and Perils of Technology). Rosen Publishing Group, 2020.

Oxlade, Chris. *Computer Science for Curious Kids: An Illustrated Introduction to Software Programming, Artificial Intelligence, Cyber-Security—and More!* Arcturus, 2023.

Small, Cathleen. *How to Choose Your Perfect Computer Science Career* (STEM Career Choices). Cheriton Children's Books, 2023.

Weakland, Mark. *How Does Wi-Fi Work?* (High Tech Science at Home). Capstone Global Library, 2021.

Websites

Discover more about how Wi-Fi works at:
https://computer.howstuffworks.com/wireless-network.htm

Find out more about Wi-Fi at:
https://kids.britannica.com/students/article/Wi-Fi/545141

Discover more facts about Wi-Fi at:
https://kids.kiddle.co/Wi-Fi

Publisher's note to educators and parents:
All the websites featured above have been carefully reviewed to ensure that they are suitable for students. However, many websites change often, and we cannot guarantee that a site's future contents will continue to meet our high standards of educational value. Please be advised that students should be closely monitored whenever they access the Internet.

INDEX

ABOUT THE AUTHOR

Kelly Roberts has written many children's science and technology books. Wi-Fi technology has made it possible for her to research and write this book from just about anywhere.